STUDY GUIDES

English

Year

3

LES RAY AND GILL BUDGELL

Contents

RISING STARS

Content grid

🚦 = Assess your understanding

Links to Primary Framework for Literacy Year 3

	Unit title	Focus text	Strand	Strand objective	Chat challenge
1	Prefixes	Examples of prefixes: *un-, de-, dis-, re-, pre-*	6 Word structure and spelling	Recognise a range of prefixes and suffixes, understanding how they modify meaning and spelling, and how they assist in decoding long complex words	Check understanding of terminology, purpose and links to spelling and meaning
2	Suffixes	From *The Pied Piper of Hamelin* by Robert Browning			
3	Plurals	Reference book			
4	🚦 What have we learned?				
5	Making notes	Skateboarding		Identify and make notes of the main points of section(s) of text	Check understanding of purpose and techniques
6	Characters and their feelings	From *The Girl Who Stayed for Half a Week* by Gene Kemp		Infer characters' feelings in fiction and consequences in logical explanations	Explore a wider discussion about characters in books read as well as how we understand character
7	Finding your way around reference texts	A dictionary page	7 Understanding and interpreting texts (9 creating and shaping texts)	Identify how different texts are organised, including reference texts, magazines and leaflets on paper and on screen. *(Write non-narrative texts using structures of different text types)*	Explore a wider discussion about fiction and non-fiction texts Check on terminology
8	Letters	Letters			Use as a basis for discussion about purpose and audience
9	Leaflets	Rutland Water Butterfly Farm leaflet			Use as a basis for discussion about information and persuasion
10	Instructions	The line trick			Use as a basis for discussion about the features of instructional texts
11	Descriptive words	From *Charmed Life* by Diana Wynne Jones		Use syntax, context and word structure to build their store of vocabulary as they read for meaning. *(Select and use a range of technical and descriptive vocabulary)*	Check understanding of terminology and purpose

	Unit title	Focus text	Strand	Strand objective	Chat challenge
12	Characters with a problem	From *Secrets* by Anita Desai	8 Engaging with and responding to texts	Empathise with characters and debate moral dilemmas portrayed in texts	Use as a basis to discuss characters in personal reading. What is a 'problem'?
13	Shape poems	'How Playtime Shapes Up' by Chris Ogden		Identify features that writers use to provoke readers' reactions	Discuss the nature of poetry and the children's experiences
14	**⊟ What have we learned?**				
15	Correct order	Cartoon from *Mr Croc Gets Fit* by Frank Rogers	9 Creating and shaping texts	Use beginning, middle and end to write narratives in which events are sequenced logically and conflicts resolved	Discuss the importance of sequence and order
16	Beginnings	'Magic Cat' by Peter Dixon			Discuss the importance of beginnings. What are the children's experiences of 'good' beginnings?
17	Planning your story	'Soupy Boy' by Damon Burnard			Revisit the purpose of planning and the range of techniques
18	Endings	'Big Bad Raps' by Tony Mitton			Discuss the importance of endings. What are the children's experiences of 'good' endings?
19	Time and place	Cartoon story	10 Text structure and organisation	Signal sequence, place and time to give coherence	Check on understanding of terminology, usage and purpose
20	Paragraphs	*The Sun and The Wind*, a fable by Aesop		Group related material into paragraphs	
21	Beginning new paragraphs	Visit to the British Museum			
22	**⊟ What have we learned?**				
23	Full stops or commas?	From *Little Grey Rabbit's Birthday* by Alison Uttley	11 Sentence structure and punctuation	Clarify meaning through the use of exclamation marks and speech marks	Check on understanding of punctuation terminology
24	Punctuation of speech	From *Loud Emily* by Alexis O'Neill			
25	Using connectives	Bicycle safety		Show relationships of time, reason and cause through subordination and connectives	Check on understanding of connectives. Use the Handy Hints section for guidance
26	Writing sentences using adjectives	From *Josie Smith at Christmas* by Magdalen Nabb		Compose sentences using adjectives, verbs and nouns for precision, clarity and impact	Check on understanding of grammar terminology, purpose and effect
27	Writing sentences using verbs	From *The Gigantic Badness* by Janet McNeill			
28	**⊟ What have we learned?**				

1 Prefixes

What happens to the spelling of words when you add prefixes?
Let's investigate!

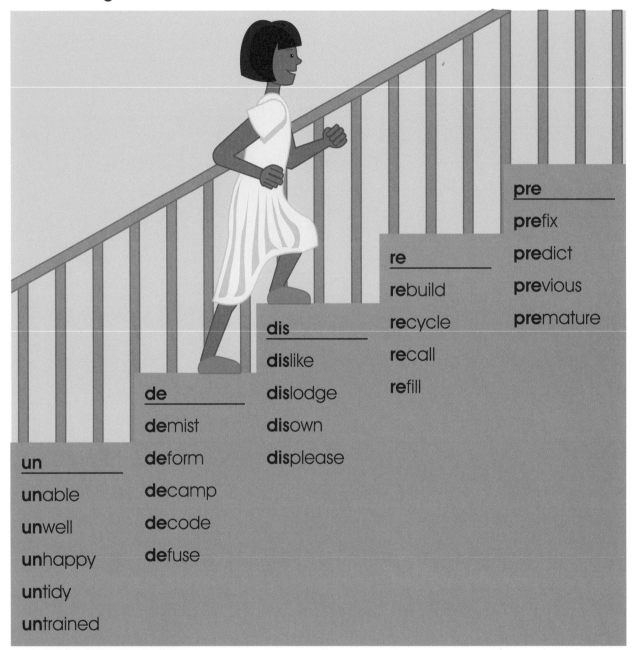

pre
prefix
predict
previous
premature

re
rebuild
recycle
recall
refill

dis
dislike
dislodge
disown
displease

de
demist
deform
decamp
decode
defuse

un
unable
unwell
unhappy
untidy
untrained

Chat challenge

What is a **prefix**?

What does the prefix *pre-* mean?

How does knowing this tell you what a prefix does?

Does adding prefixes change the meaning of a word? Explain how.

Are there any words that you do not understand? Use a dictionary to find their meanings.

Comprehension

1) Prefixes mean something. You can tell this by looking at what the words on the opposite page have in common. What do you think *re-* means?

2) How does adding *un-* to a word change its meaning?

3) Try saying the words opposite without the prefix. Which are no longer complete words? Does this happen in any one group?

4) Which words in the list opposite mean these phrases?

   not feeling healthy   to make something again   to tell the future

Objective focus

1) Add the prefix *dis-* to the following words. Write the words and check the spelling. Does the original word change its spelling?

   a. qualify   **b.** agree   **c.** appear   **d.** connect

2) Add the prefix *re-* to the following words. Write the words and check the spelling. Does the original word change its spelling?

   a. place   **b.** visit   **c.** play   **d.** write

3) Choose the correct prefix: *un-*, *dis-* or *de-* to add to the following words. Write the words and check the spelling.

   a. frost   **b.** lucky   **c.** compose   **d.** obey   **e.** popular

4) Use a dictionary. Find two new words containing the prefix *un-* and four new words with the prefix *re-*. Write the words and check the spelling.

Links to writing

1) Which of the following words have the wrong prefix? Write the words correctly. Check the spelling.

   a. disofficial   **b.** uninfect   **c.** unusual   **d.** detreat

   e. dispare   **f.** dishonest   **g.** deflate   **h.** return

2) Write some rules about prefixes to help when writing.

   What are they? How can they help with word meanings?

   How do they help with spelling?

   Do they change the spelling of words when you add them?

2 Suffixes

**What happens to the spelling of verbs when *-ing* is added?
Let's investigate!**

In The Pied Piper of Hamelin, *Robert Browning tells the story of how a Piper leads away all the children in the town. He plays music and the children follow. Here are some lines from the poem.*

Adapted from *The Pied Piper of Hamelin*

Small feet were patter**ing**, wooden shoes clatter**ing**,

Little hands clapp**ing**, and little tongues chatter**ing**,

Out came all the children runn**ing**.

All the little boys and girls,

With rosy cheeks and golden curls,

And sparkl**ing** eyes and teeth like pearls,

Tripp**ing** and skipp**ing**, ran merrily after

The wonderful music with shouting and laughter.

Chat challenge

What is a **suffix**?

Where do you find them in words?

Which suffix is in **bold** in the poem?

Which type of words is it being added to?

Does the spelling of the original words change when you add a suffix?

Which words do you not know the meaning of? Find their meanings in a dictionary.

Comprehension

1) What were the small feet doing?

2) What kind of shoes are these children wearing?

3) The poet says that the children are like 'fowl in the farmyard' as they run into the street. Write down the name of two kinds of animals that we call **fowl**.

4) Write what we are told about.

Their hair	Their complexion	Their eyes	Their teeth

You might need to use a dictionary. Give the answer in your own words.

5) List at least two verbs that the poet uses to show how the children moved.

Objective focus

Add the suffix *-ing* to the following verbs. Write the words and check the spelling. Does the original verb change its spelling? Say how.

a. jump   **b.** push   **c.** throw   **d.** help

e. sail   **f.** write   **g.** hope   **h.** take

i. drive   **j.** run   **k.** skip   **l.** swim

Links to writing

1) Write five more examples of your own where:

a. adding *-ing* does not change the spelling of the original word, e.g. **chatter → chattering**

b. you have to drop the final -e in the verb, e.g. **sparkle → sparkling**

c. you have to double the final letter in the verb, e.g. **skip → skipping**.

2) Think about what you have investigated about adding the suffix *-ing*. Write three rules for a poster about spelling words with *-ing* at the end, giving examples. Use the computer.

3 Plurals

What happens to the spelling of some nouns when you make them plural? Let's investigate!

	Take one plant.		There are many flowering plants.
	A seed grows into a new plant.		Flowering plants grow many seeds.
	Poppies have seeds in seed pods which dry out.		Some seed pods explode and scatter the seeds in all directions!
	A dandelion 'clock' is a soft, white ball of tiny, light seeds on stalks.		The seeds are so light that a puff of wind can blow them away.
	Animals can help to scatter seeds.		Birds and other animals eat blackberries and other fruits. The fruit is digested but the seeds pass through their bodies.

Chat challenge

What does **singular** mean? What does **plural** mean?

What is a noun? How many plural nouns can you find here?

What happens to the spelling of most nouns when you make them plural?

Comprehension

1) What kind of book do you think this text is from?
2) Why do flowering plants grow seeds?
3) Why do the seeds need to travel?
4) Give two examples of how seeds can be spread around by the plant.
5) How can animals help to scatter seeds?

Objective focus

1) Write the plurals of the following words. What happens to their spelling?

   a. book   **b.** desk   **c.** pencil   **d.** pen

2) Write the plurals of the following words. What sort of sound does the word end in? Do they have an extra syllable?

   a. bush   **b.** glass   **c.** watch   **d.** inch

3) What happens to most words ending in -x? Investigate the plurals of these words and write them. What sort of sound does the word end in?

   a. fox   **b.** box   **c.** tax   **d.** fax

4) Write the plurals of the following words. What happens to their spelling?

   a. army   **b.** jelly   **c.** puppy   **d.** party

5) You might think these words would follow the same rule – but they don't. Write their plurals. What is different about them? Clue: look at the last two letters!

   a. donkey   **b.** boy   **c.** delay   **d.** key

Links to writing

1) Find and write five words of your own to show what you have learned about the five different ways nouns can make plurals.
2) Imagine that a new person has arrived in your class who does not speak English very well. Write a set of 'handy hints' with examples, to help him or her to spell plurals correctly.

   Provide some rules. Give examples for each.
   Suggest ways of remembering them.
   Don't forget the ones that break the rules!

Assess your understanding

 OK

 OK but need more practice

 not at all clear and need to revisit

4 What have we learned?

We've learned about **word structure and spelling**.

1 How prefixes can help us to spell and understand the meaning of words

- A prefix is a letter pattern fixed to the beginning of a word which affects its meaning.
- If you know what the prefix means, it can help you to work out the meaning of an unknown word and how to spell it.
- Just add the prefix and do not change the spelling of the word.

Check understanding!

Make a chart like this to help you remember the meaning of useful prefixes.

Prefix	Meaning	Example word
un-	not	undo
de-	making the opposite of	decode
dis-	not	dislike
re-	again	
pre-	before	

2 How to add -*ing* to help us to spell and understand the meaning of words

- A suffix is a letter pattern fixed to the end of a word which affects its meaning.
- Most words just add -*ing* to the verb.
- If the word ends in -e then drop the -e and add -*ing*, e.g. **hope** → **hoping**.
- If the word has a short vowel sound in it then the last consonant will double before you add -*ing*, e.g. **stop** → **stopping**.

Assess your understanding OK  OK but need more practice 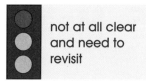 not at all clear and need to revisit

Check understanding!

 Make a chart like this for *-ing* and add more suffixes to it as you learn them. Ask for help if you need it.

Suffix	Rule	But remember ...
-ing	Just add *-ing*	**hope** changes to **hoping** **run** changes to **running**
-er	Just add *-er*	**nicer** not **niceer** **happier** not **happyer** **bigger** not **biger**
-est		
-y		
-ly		

> If a word ends in a hissing, buzzing and shushing sound, add *-es*.

3 How understanding about singular and plurals can help us to spell words

- **Singular** means *one* and **plural** means *more than one*.
- Most words add *-s*, e.g. **dogs**.
- Words ending in vowel + *-y* add *-s*, e.g. **keys**.
- Words ending in *-y* change to *i* and add *-es*, e.g. **cities**.
- Words ending in *-x* usually add *-es*, e.g. **boxes**.
- Words ending in *-e* just add *-s*, e.g. **games**.

Check understanding!

 Write a test for a friend. Think of one word for each of the four rules above and see if you can catch someone out!

Test yourself too!

5 Making notes

Skateboarding

Skateboarding started in the 1930s. Children attached roller skates to a wooden plank. In 1958 the first real skateboard was made in California. Firstly, the shop owner made sets of skate wheels. Then he attached them to square wooden boards. Soon, many young people were rolling down hills and calling it 'sidewalk surfing'.

The first skateboarding competition was held at a middle school in California in 1964. In 1965, the first National Skateboard Championship was on the TV. In 1966, the first film was made showing only skateboarders doing tricks. This was called 'Skater Dater'.

By the 1970s over 40 million skateboards were sold in America. Lots of skate parks were opened. A man named Guy Grundy set the speed record on a skateboard of 68 mph.

Chat challenge

Why do people make notes?

Are notes always written in complete sentences?

Is it important to write in your own words?

How do people use short forms of words when they write notes?

Can you think of any examples?

How else do people make notes?

Comprehension

1) When did skateboarding start?

2) Where was the first real skateboard made?

3) What did young people first call this sport?

4) List three important things about skateboards that happened in the 1960s.

5) How do you know that skateboarding was an important sport by 1970?

6) Who set the speed record? How fast did he go?

Objective focus

1) To make notes, you must find important facts from each paragraph. You can make notes by asking yourself questions: What? Who? When? How? Why? Answer them as briefly as possible, e.g. *When did skateboarding start? Started 1950s.* Complete a chart to help.

Paragraph	Important facts about skateboarding
1	Started 1950 – roller skate wheels on wooden planks 1958 – California – surfers used first real boards – 'sidewalk surfing'
2	

2) It is important to use your own words – not just copy the passage. Write the following in your own words, using as few as possible.

  a. Children attached roller skates to a wooden plank.

  b. Many young people were rolling down hills and calling it 'sidewalk surfing'.

3. In notes, people shorten words, e.g. **and** *is sometimes written as* **&.** What short words could you use for:

  a. *first*   **b.** *middle*   **c.** *school*   **d.** *park*?

Links to writing

1) Choose another passage from a book you are using in class, such as a history topic. Make notes in a chart like the one above and ask the questions as above too.

2) Carry out a class survey. See how many other ways there are of making notes, such as using spider-diagrams or highlighting main points on a photocopy.

6 Characters and their feelings

From *The Girl Who Stayed for Half a Week*

Some kids hate their teacher. I nearly hated Miss Baker last year. She always put me down. Look where you're putting your feet, Michael, must your work be so untidy, so messy, Michael, do you have to take up so much room, Michael? I couldn't help being me and sprouting in all directions. I couldn't help growing. I didn't tell myself to grow. I just did. But in the end I didn't hate her … In fact I gave her a box of chocolates at the end of the year, though I didn't choose my favourites and five other kids gave her the same kind.

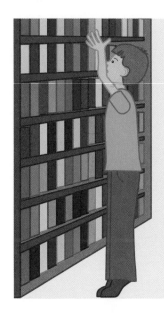

But Miss is something else. If Miss reads something you've written and she thinks it's good she smiles at the pages before she says anything as if she understands the meaning behind the words you wrote on the page, sad or frightening or funny. She's got grey eyes and curly brown hair and a curly grin with a crooked tooth and she's not very big so I reach things down from the shelves for her, being the tallest in the class, although Greg Grubber is wider.

Gene Kemp

Chat challenge

Why do writers include characters in their stories?

Why is it important to tell your reader about how these characters feel?

How can you tell how a character feels?

Through how he or she acts?

What he or she says?

How he or she behaves?

Can you think of examples of these from books that you have read?

Comprehension

1) What is the name of the main character of this story?

2) Why did he hate his teacher for a time?

3) What was the problem as he was growing up?

4) Why did he change what he thought about Miss Baker?

5) How did he show this at the end of the year?

6) Michael says he didn't choose his favourites. What does this show about him?

 Objective focus

1) Using the right words is important if you are trying to show how a character feels. Make two columns with the headings **Feels happy** and **Feels sad**. Put the following words in the correct column. Look up any words that you do not understand.

blissful	wretched	elated	desolate	lively
anguished	distressed	jovial	mournful	joyous

2) Use the words in sentences about characters to show that you know what they mean. How would characters act if they felt like this?

3) Write the story from Greg Grubber's point of view. How does he feel about his size? How do people make fun of him? How does he try to get Miss Baker's attention?

 Links to writing

1) Continue the story of Michael and Miss Baker. Show how they become even better friends and why Michael ends up giving her a box of chocolates at the end of the year! Michael could produce an excellent piece of work and Miss Baker might encourage him to put it on the school website.

What would Greg Grubber say and do?

How would she persuade Michael?

What happens when the writing is published?

Why does Michael give Miss Baker his favourite chocolates in the end?

7 Finding your way around reference texts

Let's find out more about reference texts.

Sometimes you have to look up the meaning of hard words. You can look in a *dictionary* or a *thesaurus*.

A **dictionary** is arranged in **alphabetical order**

> **massage** 1 *n.* act of rubbing or stroking to relieve aches and pains
> 2 *v.* to perform massage
> **massive** 1 *adj.* forming or consisting of a large mass
> 2. *adj.* large of scope or degree
> **mast** 1 *n.* long pole rising from deck of a ship from which sail can be set
> 2 *n.* vertical pole supporting radio or TV aerial
> 3 *v.* to equip with a mast

It gives the **definitions** (meanings) of words

It helps us **check the spelling** of **words**

A **thesaurus** is also arranged in **alphabetical order**

> **director** instructor, ruler, controller, adviser, manager, master, superintendent, leader, monitor, guide
> **dirt** filth, foulness, sordidness, uncleanness, soil, muck, grime, mud
> **dirty** filthy, foul, sordid, unclean, soiled, mucky, grimy, begrimed, sullied, nasty, squalid

It contains **synonyms** (words with similar meanings)

Chat challenge

Why do people use reference books?

What kinds of reference books do you use at school?

Do you use any reference books at home? What kinds?

How are they different from other books in the way they look on the page?

Where else could you look to find out about meanings of words?

Comprehension

1) How is a dictionary arranged? How does this help us to find words?

2) What two things can it help us with?

3) List two other things dictionaries tell us about words.

4) How is a thesaurus arranged?

5) How is it different from a dictionary in what it tries to do?

6) What is a **synonym**?

 Objective focus

1) Imagine that **skin** and **slot** are the first and last words on a dictionary page. Which words from this list would you find on the page? Write them in alphabetical order.

slum	slang	leigh	skull	slope	skirt	snake	skate
sober	skewer	skid	sloop	slave	slither	social	smile

2) Find a word from the box that has the most similar meaning to each of these.

a. reveal

b. prohibit

c. jovial

boats	show	hide	meat	forbid
jolly	allow	sad	quiet	reserved

3) Find a word from the box that has the opposite meaning to these.

a. absent

b. ancient

c. cautious

stupid	present	disappeared	old
modern	often	reckless	curse	help

 Links to writing

1) Choose ten words from the activities above that you had to look up in a dictionary or thesaurus. Write them in sentences to show that you understand what they mean.

2) Make up an alphabet quiz to use in class, e.g. *What letter makes honey?* (B). *Which letter allows ships to sail?* (C).

8 Letters

Let's investigate letters for a range of different purposes.

Letter 1

The New School,
Bird Lane,
London, N11 11A

30 March 2007

The Manager
Naff Coaches Ltd
Neasden

Dear Sir,

I am writing to complain about poor service from your coach service last week.

My class (3B) were going on a day trip to the Natural History Museum. We only go on three trips a year and everyone was ready to leave at 8.30 a.m.

The coach had been booked by our teacher, Ms Sharpe, three months ago and you were told the time to arrive.

You did not arrive until 10.30 a.m. When you did arrive you did not apologise. You just said that 'there had been a problem'. Many of the boys and girls in my class were disappointed. All you did was to tell them off about making too much noise and eating sweets on the coach.

When we arrived at the museum we were too late for our special talk and so missed the best bits about dinosaurs.

What I want to know is what you are going to do about this? All my class were very upset. We had to pay for the trip but we did not get there in time.

I look forward to your reply.

Yours sincerely,

Mina Patel

Mina Patel

Letter 2

School – 31 March 2007

Hi Sophie,

Just had to tell you what happened yesterday – what a mess! You know Ms Sharpe takes us to the museum every year – usually a big yawn – ugh! But it was such a laugh this year.

First the coach didn't turn up. We were waiting hours – and most of us ate our sandwiches. Of course the teachers were going mad. When it did arrive the driver was a real misery guts – all he did was moan, moan, moan ... we all had a laugh on the coach though with Fred's new iPod. Much better listening to the music.

The museum was good, even though we missed the bit with the dinosaurs. Now we're back in school and have to do all that writing! I have to stop Fred copying my work – he never does anything for himself.

Anyway – talk soon. Love n'stuff,

Mina

Chat challenge

Why do people write letters?

Who would be the audience for these letters?

What do you notice about the layout of the letters?

Comprehension

1) Who is Letter 1 written to? What is its purpose?

2) What happened to make Mina write the letter? Give some examples to prove your point.

3) Which part of the trip were the children really looking forward to?

4) What do you think she expects the coach company to do?

5) Who is Letter 2 written to? What is its purpose?

6) Why is Mina writing this letter? Give some examples to prove your point.

7) What does Letter 2 say about how Mina felt about school trips?

Objective focus

1) Compare the style and layout of the two letters. Use a chart like this one.

	Letter 1	Letter 2
Purpose		
Tone (how it sounds)	serious, concerned	friendly, jokey
Layout		
Language used		

2) Write out these addresses correctly for letters. What rules about setting out addresses can you think of?

   a. 3 lisburne rd belfast nn3 2ds

   b. home farm mill st ambridge borsetshire bs3 2ss

   c. flat 6 docklands buildings admirals sq London w1 2ww

Links to writing

1) Imagine that you bought a new computer game and it does not work. Write a letter to the company that made it, explaining that you want to replace it. You could use the computer to write and print it.

2) Write a letter to a penfriend who lives overseas, explaining all about your new game and what happened when you realised that it did not work.

9 Leaflets

5,000 square feet of
jungle paradise

The largest tropical house
in the area

Walk amongst beautifully
coloured butterflies and
lots of other animals too.

We are situated on Sykes Lane Car park, on the
A606 Oakham to Stamford Road, near the village
of Empingham. Tourist signposted from the road.

Why not visit us soon?

The Butterfly Farm
Sykes Lane Car Park, Empingham
North Shore Rutland Water
Oakham, Rutland LE15 8PX
Tel & Fax: 01780 460515
www.rutlandwaterbutterflyfarm.co.uk
Schools and other groups are our
speciality. Please call for details.
Open every day from 1st April until
31st October from 10.30-17.00
last admissions half an hour before closing
10.30-16.30 in September and October

Rutland Water Butterfly Farm

From the heart of
England, to the heart of
the jungle.....a totally
tropical treat

An amazing world of contrasts awaits you

From babbling brook to the mighty reservoir, all the fish of the
area are housed in the impressive Aquatic Centre.

Here can you see at close quarters the huge Carp of the lake
as well as all the other coarse and game fish of the area in one
of the finest freshwater Aquariums.

In the Aquatic Centre, the hidden world of Rutland Water is
no longer hidden.

inside the 5,000 square feet
of tropical jungle

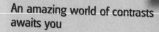

part of the aquatic display

Inside the Tropical House

Walk through the doors and be transported into five
thousand square feet of tropical paradise. Hundreds of
brilliantly coloured butterflies fly around you whilst the
parrots and other birds look on.

In the ponds, large Koi carp swim around whilst the
terrapins sun themselves on the sides.

Look for the Iguana lizards up in the trees and many
other animals such as stick insects and Giant African land
Snails in the undergrowth.

The tropical house is designed with everybody in
mind, prams and wheelchairs will have no problems on
our completely flat slabbed pathways.

A great visit - everytime

Young and old alike will be enthralled by this
magical environment. Will you be lucky enough to
see the marvel of a butterfly emerging from its
pupa? Maybe one will even land on your head.
One thing is for sure, no two visits are the same.
Maybe this is why visitors return time and again.

The Twilight Zone

Our newest attraction. Safely housed behind
glass are some of the world's mini-beasts. From
huge tarantula spiders to poisonous scorpions...
dare you enter? Will you leave wanting to cuddle
a cockroach?

Other facilities

We have a large car park and just yards from the
centre you will find a cafe, children's adventure playground and toilets. Don't forget Europe's largest man
made lake, with all that has to offer.

Chat challenge

What is a leaflet?

Why do people write them?

Where do you get leaflets from?

What do you notice is different about the layout of a leaflet from
other kinds of text?

Comprehension

1) Who is this leaflet aimed at? What does it aim to do?

2) What does the writer mean by 'a world of contrasts'?

3) Where are all the fish living at this farm?

4) Use a dictionary to find the meaning of these hard words.

   a. babbling   **b.** reservoir   **c.** impressive   **d.** aquatic   **e.** paradise

5) How large is the 'jungle paradise'?

Objective focus

1) Investigate the features of leaflets. Draw and complete a chart.

Feature	Example
Audience	
Big, bold text	
Short paragraphs	
Use of pictures	
Main headings or headlines	
Talks to you	

2) Why do you think pictures are used in this leaflet? What information do they add? How do they make the leaflet appealing to the audience?

3) Write the words and phrases that would persuade you to go to the butterfly farm. Say why.

Links to writing

1) Design and write a leaflet about a local place you know – a park, theme park or a sea-life centre.

   Who is your audience? What are you trying to do?

   Where will you find the right information? Who will you ask?

   What features will be important in the design?

   You could use the computer to design and print the leaflet – and even try it out on any new pupils.

10 Instructions

What do you need to know in order to write good instructions?
Let's investigate!

The line trick

Follow these instructions and you will be able to convince your friends that they cannot believe their eyes!

You'll need a pencil, a piece of paper and a ruler.

1 Draw two lines the same length. Label the lines **A** and **B**.

Line **A**   Line **B**

2 Draw lines at the top and bottom of the first line (Line A), like this:

3 Draw lines at the top and bottom of the other line (Line B), like this:

4 Show people the lines, side by side.

Say, 'Is Line **A** or Line **B** the longer, or are the two lines the same length?'

Most people think Line **B** is longer. They are wrong! The lines at the top and bottom just make it look longer. Let them measure the lines to show that they are the same length.

Chat challenge

Why might we need to use instructions?
What would we be trying to do?
How is the layout of instructions often different from other kinds of text?
Do these features help in making instructions better? How?

Comprehension

1) What is the aim of these instructions?

2) How long should you draw the first two lines?

3) What are you told to add to these two lines after this?

4) What do people think when they see the lines?

5) How do they test that they are wrong?

6) How many instructions are you given? How do you know this?

Objective focus

1) Investigate the features of instructions. Copy and complete a chart like this.

Feature	Example
What is the aim?	
What do you need?	
What are the steps?	
How do you know?	
What kinds of verbs are used?	Commands: **Draw** lines … **show** people …
Who is being given the instructions?	

Links to writing

1) Write a set of instructions explaining how to make something, such as a paper aeroplane.

   Why are you making it? What do you need to make it?

   How will you make it – step by step?

   How will you test whether it works?

   Which other features will you use?

2) Write other kinds of instructions, e.g. how to find your way from school to home, to give to a new friend who is visiting.

   Do you use different features?

   How important is it to get the facts correct and in the right order?

   Will a diagram be helpful?

11 Descriptive words

Different kinds of words that you use help to make a picture in your reader's mind. Let's look at some of these.

From *Charmed Life*

The door of the room sprang open of its own accord and the **huge** spider went silently creeping towards it, swaying on its **hairy** legs. It squeezed its legs inward to get through the door, and crept onwards, down the passage beyond.

Gwendolen touched the other creatures, one by one. The earwigs lumbered up and off, like **shiny horned** cows, **bright brown** and glistening. The frogs rose up, as big as men, and walked flap, flop on their **enormous** feet, and with their arms trailing like gorillas. Their **mottled** skin quivered, and little holes kept opening and shutting. The **puffy** place under their chins made gulping movements. The black beetle crawled on branched legs, such a **big, black** slab that it could barely get through the door. Cat could see it, and all the others, going in **slow, silent** procession down the **grass-green, glowing** corridor.

Diana Wynne Jones

Chat challenge

What is an **adjective**? Look at the words in bold.
What is a **verb**?
Why is it important to use descriptive words in your writing?
What would your writing be like if you didn't? How would your audience react?

Comprehension

1) How do you know the door of the room opened fast?

2) What came through it? How did it move?

3) Which words tell you it was so large that it was a tight fit?

4) What do the earwigs remind the author of?

5) What was surprising about the size of the frogs? Find some evidence.

6) Explain how all these creatures moved down the corridor.

Objective focus

1) Read the extract aloud without the adjectives in bold. What difference does it make?

2) Replace some of the adjectives with your own, e.g. **huge spider** → **large spider**. Talk about which word gives a better description. Why?

3) Find the adverbs used in the passage. What do they add that is extra to the description? If you took them away, would it make a difference?

4) 'Flap, flop' describes the sound made by the frog. You can hear it because of the words. Write sentences using your own sound words to describe these:

   a. the breaking of a window

   b. moving water in a washing machine

   c. leaves on a tree blowing in the wind.

Links to writing

1) Continue the story. Write about what happens next. What will the creatures do? Will Gwendolen change them back? How will the story end?

   Use words to help you make the scene come alive.

   Which of your senses will be involved? Use sound words.

   Choose adjectives and adverbs carefully.

   Use vivid verbs – not boring ones. Look in a thesaurus.

2) Imagine that you are a wizard or a witch. One of your spells goes wrong. Write a story about what happens.

12 Characters with a problem

Rohan has found a magic rubber, but he gets carried away when his mother gets angry …

From *Secrets*

His mother was so angry, she shouted, 'What's the matter with you, you rascal? Look what you have done! What a mess you've made. Now go and fetch the broom and sweep it up at once.'

'I won't sweep,' he shouted back, as loudly as though there were a devil in him, shouting for him.

She was still more angry. 'I won't sweep it up either. Let it lie there, and then your father will see it when he comes home,' she said.

Then Rohan felt so afraid that he held up the magic rubber and cried, 'I won't let you do that. I won't let him see it. I'll – I'll rub you all out,' and he swept through the air with the little grey lump of rubber, as hard as he could. He shut his eyes tight because his face was all screwed up with anger, and when he opened them the whole house with the unlit fire, the brass pan, the glass of milk and even his mother had vanished. There was only the roof-top, blazing in the afternoon sun, littered with empty tins and old tyres at the edges but quite, quite bare in the middle.

Now Rohan did not have a home or a mother or even a glass of milk. His mouth hung open, he was so frightened by what he had done.

Anita Desai

Chat challenge

What's the problem here?
Can you think of any stories with characters who have a problem?
How do they solve their problems?
What would the story be like if the main character did not have a problem to solve?

Comprehension

1) Explain why Rohan's mother was angry.

2) What did she ask him to do as a result?

3) What was Rohan really afraid of?

4) Why did he 'shut his eyes tight' when he used the rubber?

5) What three things did he think of immediately when he had rubbed out the scene?

6) How did he feel when he knew what he had done? How do we know this by his actions?

Objective focus

1) Do you think Rohan was to blame for his problem? Draw two columns with the headings **To blame** and **Not to blame**. Think of arguments. Write in each column. Talk about this with a partner. Do they have different ideas?

2) Who do you feel more sorry for – Rohan or his mother? Write a paragraph beginning: 'I feel sorry for Rohan because …' Now write one about feeling sorry for his mother.

3) Describe why you think Rohan got into this trouble. What kind of character was he? Would you have done the same? What could he have done to avoid it?

4) Imagine that Rohan writes a letter of apology to his mother (when she comes back). What would it say?

Links to writing

1) Continue the story of Rohan's problem.
   How does Rohan solve his problem? How do other people feel about him now?
   What does his father say and do? What does this show about his character?

2) Write about another time when something happens that he rubs out. Think about how you will start the story.

13 Shape poems

Look carefully at these words and the help given about how to spell them.

— How Playtime Shapes Up —

to claim part of it for their own!

Every

breaktime   boys

the

play

five-a-side

across

of

the all

playground

never daring to stray away from the

walls and wondering if they'll ever be able

And all around the edge the girls stand,

Chris Ogden

Chat challenge

Is this really a poem? Give your reasons.

What do you notice about the shape?

How do the words make up the shape?

What do you like about it?

Would it have been better written in lines like a 'normal' poem?

Comprehension

1) What do the boys do in the playground? When do they do this? Where?

2) What do the girls do? Why?

3) Why do you think they don't dare to 'stray away from the walls'?

4) What do the girls hope for?

5) Is this the kind of thing that happens in your school?

6) Do you think it is right? What would you do about it?

Objective focus

1) What shapes does the poem make? How do the words help to make the shapes? Does the shape match the subject?

2) Read the poem aloud. Then write the words of the poem without the shape. Read this version aloud. What difference does the shape make to the poem?

3) The words of the poem are simple. Add adjectives to every noun. Add adverbs to every verb. Choose new verbs. What difference does this make? Use a chart to help.

Adjective	Noun	Verb	Adverb
excited	boys	scrabble	energetically

4) Rewrite the poem using these new words. Which version do you like better? Why? Which version makes the better shape? Why?

Links to writing

1) Write other shape poems about football.
   What idea do you want to give your reader about football?
   List words you can think of – adjectives and verbs.
   What shape will make your reader think about football?
   Make the words fit the shape – or make the words into shapes.

2) Design and write a shape poem about autumn.
   List adjectives and verbs for autumn.
   Draw outlines of leaves falling from a tree. Make big leaf shapes.
   Write the words on the leaves.

Assess your understanding **OK**

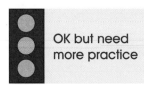 **OK but need more practice**

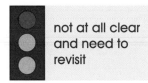 **not at all clear and need to revisit**

14 What have we learned?

We've learned about **understanding and interpreting texts** and **how to engage and respond to texts**.

1 How and why we make notes

- Notes should highlight the most important bits of information.
- Don't just copy out sentences.
- Ask … Who? What? Why? When? Why? … to check that you have found the most important bits.

Check understanding!

 Make some notes on how to behave in assembly – draw or write these.

2 How to understand a character's feelings

- Writers can use words to:
  - tell us what they think about a character or what a character is feeling
  - show us what a character does or says.

Check understanding!

 Choose a friend to write about. Write an example of what you think about your friend, what your friend does or says and how your friend is feeling.

3 How to use reference texts

- A dictionary:
  - gives **definitions** (the meaning) of words
  - gives **derivations** (where the word has come from)
  - tells us what type of word it is, e.g. *verb, noun.*
- A thesaurus gives **synonyms** (words with similar meanings).

Check understanding!

 Use a dictionary to find out how the word **verb** is shortened in a dictionary (look up **run**).

Use a thesaurus to find a synonym for **spooky**.

Assess your understanding

 OK

 OK but need more practice

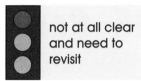 not at all clear and need to revisit

4 How information texts are organised

Letters	Leaflets	Instructions
Formal/informal	Headings and subheadings	Brief and clear
Address and date	Use of pictures or diagrams	Ordered
Beginning and ending greeting	Tells you what to think/do	Lists materials or equipment
Paragraphs	Bullet points	Tells you what to do

Check understanding!

 Who would you write a formal letter to? An informal letter to? What would you write a leaflet about? What would you write instructions for?

5 How to use clues in the text to read new vocabulary

- Read either side of the tricky word to look for clues.
- Look for linked words that you **do** understand.

Check understanding!

Look at the first sentence in your reading book. Rewrite it using different vocabulary.

6 How to understand a character's problems

- A character with a problem to solve is more interesting than one who hasn't! Check out the points under section 2 opposite.

Check understanding!

Write out a really good problem that would make an interesting read. How would you tell your reader about this problem?

7 How to notice key points about how a poem is written

- It may only use a list of words but they need to be carefully chosen and set out.

Check understanding!

 Look at other poems and make a list of other features that you notice. Use them the next time you can.

15 Correct order

From *Mr Croc Gets Fit*

Frank Rogers

Chat challenge

What is the correct order for a story? Is there one?

Why is the correct order important in stories?

What would happen if stories were not always in the correct order?

How do you know that this story is in the correct order?

Is there a way of telling this story in a different order?

RISING STARS

English Study Guide: Year 3

Answer Booklet

1 Prefixes
Comprehension
1) *Re-* means 'again'.
2) *Un-* means 'not'.
3) In the *pre-* group, *-dict* and *-vious* are not complete words.
4) unwell, rebuild, predict

Objective focus
1) The original spelling does not change.
   a. disqualify
   b. disagree
   c. disappear
   d. disconnect
2) The original spelling does not change.
   a. replace
   b. revisit
   c. replay
   d. rewrite
3) a. defrost
   b. unlucky
   c. decompose
   d. disobey
   e. unpopular
4) *Own answer*

Links to writing
1) a. unofficial
   b. disinfect
   c. correct
   d. retreat
   e. prepare
   f. correct
   g. correct
   h. correct
2) *Own answer*

2 Suffixes
Comprehension
1) pattering
2) wooden shoes
3) chickens, ducks
4) golden curls/rosy cheeks/sparkling eyes/like pearls
5) running, skipping, tripping

Objective focus
1) The original verb spelling does not change.
   a. jumping
   b. pushing
   c. throwing
   d. helping
   e. sailing
   These verbs drop the final -e.
   f. writing

g. hoping
h. taking
i. driving
These verbs double the final consonant.
j. running
k. skipping
l. swimming

Links to writing
1), 2) *Own answers*

3 Plurals
Comprehension
1) A book about plants.
2) It is the way they reproduce.
3) So the seeds can spread far from the plant.
4) *'Some seed pods explode and scatter the seeds in all directions!'* *'The seeds are so light that a puff of wind can blow them away.'*
5) Animals help scatter seeds by eating fruit, which is digested but the seeds pass through their bodies.

Objective focus
1) To make these words plural add an -s.
   a. books
   b. desks
   c. pencils
   d. pens
2) To make words ending in -ch or -ss plural add -es.
   a. bushes
   b. glasses
   c. watches
   d. inches
3) To make words ending in -x plural add -es.
   a. foxes
   b. boxes
   c. taxes
   d. faxes
4) To make words ending in -y plural, change the -y to -i and add -es.
   a. armies
   b. jellies
   c. puppies
   d. parties
5) To make words ending in a vowel then -y plural, just add -s.
   a. donkeys
   b. boys
   c. delays
   d. keys

Links to writing
1), 2) *Own answers*

5 Making notes
Comprehension
1) In the 1930s.
2) California
3) *'Sidewalk surfing'*
4) The first skateboarding competition was in 1964.
   The first National Skateboard Championship was in 1965.
   The first film showing only skateboarding tricks was in 1966.
5) Over 40 million skateboards were sold in America.
6) Guy Grundy set the speed record by travelling 68 mph.

Objective focus
1)

Paragraph	Important facts about skateboarding
1	Started 1950 – roller skate wheels on wooden planks 1958 – California – surfers used first real boards –'sidewalk surfing'
2	1964 – First competition – California 1965 – First competition on TV 1966 – First film – 'Skater Dater'
3	1970s – US – 40 million skateboards sold Guy Grundy – 68mph speed record

2) *Own answer*
3) a. 1st
   b. mdl
   c. schl
   d. prk

Links to writing
1), 2) *Own answers*

6 Characters and their feelings
Comprehension
1) Michael
2) She always put him down.
3) He took up a lot of room.
4) She appreciates the stories he wrote.
5) He gave her a box of chocolates.
6) *Own answer*

Objective focus

1)

Feels happy	Feels sad
blissful	wretched
elated	desolate
lively	anguished
jovial	distressed
joyous	mournful

2), 3) *Own answers*

Links to writing
1) *Own answers*

7 Finding your way around reference texts

Comprehension
1) Alphabetically, so that words are in a predictable order.
2) Meaning and spelling.
3) Derivations and what type of word it is.
4) Alphabetically
5) Gives synonyms, but not the actual meaning.
6) A word with a similar meaning.

Objective focus
1) skirt, skull, slang, slave, slither, sloop, slope
2) a. show
 b. forbid
 c. jolly
3) a. present
 b. modern
 c. reckless

Links to writing
1), 2) *Own answers*

8 Letters

Comprehension
1) Letter 1 is written to Naff Coaches Ltd, to complain about poor service.
2) Mina Patel wrote the letter because the coach arrived two hours late: *'everyone was ready to leave at 8.30', 'You did not arrive until 10.30'.*
3) A special talk about dinosaurs.
4) Refund some of the money paid for the coaches.
5) Letter 2 is written to Mina's friend Sophie to describe her day and entertain her.
6) Mina is writing this letter to share what happened to her: *'just had to tell you what happened'.*
7) Mina enjoyed the trip: *'it was such a laugh this year', 'we all had a laugh on the coach', 'The museum was good'.*

Objective focus

1)

	Letter 1	Letter 2
Purpose	persuade, inform	describe, entertain
Tone	serious, concerned	friendly
Layout	full address paragraphs	partial address paragraphs
Language used	formal	informal

2) 3 Lisburne Road,
Belfast,
NN3 2DS

Home Farm,
Mill Street,
Ambridge,
Borsetshire,
BS3 2SS

Flat 6,
Docklands Buildings,
Admirals Square,
London,
W1 2WW

Always use capital letters for place names and post codes.
Put each section of the address on a different line.

Links to writing
1), 2) *Own answers*

9 Leaflets

Comprehension
1) The leaflet is aimed at possible visitors to inform them about the farm and persuade them to come.
2) Different types of environments close together.
3) The Aquatic Centre
 a. To make continuous, murmuring sounds.
 b. A place where water is collected and stored for use.
 c. Having the ability to impress the mind.
 d. Of, in, or pertaining to water.
 e. A place of extreme beauty, delight, or happiness.
4) 5000 square feet

Objective focus

1)

Feature	Example
Audience	Why not visit us soon?
Big, bold text	A great visit – everytime
Short paragraphs	In the ponds, large Koi carp swim around whilst the terrapins sun themselves on the sides.
Use of pictures	Lots of pictures of butterflies
Main headings or headlines	The Twilight Zone

2) Pictures are used to give the reader an idea of what the farm is like, allowing them to imagine themselves there and making it more likely for them to visit.

3) *Own answer*

Links to writing
1) *Own answer*

10 Instructions

Comprehension
1) The aim of the instructions is teaching how to perform the line trick.
2) The same length.
3) Lines at the top and bottom of the lines.
4) *'Most people think Line B is longer.'*
5) By measuring the lines themselves.
6) Four steps because of the numbered steps.

Objective focus

1)

Feature	Example
What is the aim?	To perform the line trick.
What do you need?	Pencil, a piece of paper and a ruler.
What are the steps?	Draw two lines the same length.
How do you know?	There are illustrations.
What kind of verbs are used?	Commands: **Draw** lines … **show** people …
Who is being given the instructions?	Anyone reading them and wanting to learn the trick.

Links to writing
1), 2) *Own answers*

11 Descriptive words

Comprehension
1) The door *'sprang open'.*
2) A spider *'went silently creeping …'.*
3) *'huge', 'squeezed'*
4) *'shiny horned cows'*
5) The frogs were *'as big as men'* with *'enormous feet'.*
6) They moved in a *'slow, silent procession'.*

Objective focus
1) It is more difficult to make a picture in your mind.
2) *Own answer*
3) The adverbs *'silently'* and *'barely'* give extra description to the verb.
4) *Own answer*

Links to writing
1), 2) *Own answers*

12 Characters with a problem

Comprehension
1) He made a mess in the house.
2) She wanted him to sweep the mess up quickly.
3) His father being angry with him.
4) He shut his eyes because *'his face was all screwed up with anger'.*
5) He no longer had a home, his mother or milk.
6) *'He was frightened'.* We know this because *'his mouth hung open'.*

Objective focus
1), 2), 3), 4) *Own answers*

Links to writing
1), 2) *Own answers*

13 Shape poems
Comprehension
1) At playtime the boys play five-a-side on the playground.
2) The girls stand on the edge because they don't dare stray away.
3) Maybe the girls don't want to get involved in the boys' rough games.
4) *'to claim part of it for their own'*
5), 6) *Own answers*

Objective focus
1) The poem makes the shape of a playground, surrounded by walls.
2), 3), 4) *Own answers*

Links to writing
1), 2) *Own answers*

15 Correct order
Comprehension
1) From television
2) Stretch up/Run on the spot/Touch your toes
3) Touching his toes makes him burp.
4) There is a text box saying 'NEXT MORNING'.
5) Because he's still wearing his pyjamas.
6) Even though he remembers the other things he forgets to change out of his pyjamas.

Objective focus
1), 2), 3) *Own answers*

Links to writing
1), 2) *Own answers*

16 Beginnings
Comprehension
1) Tibby, Mother, Dad and the author.
2) Mum causes the problem by spilling magic.
3) The cat turned magic *'straight away'*.
4) Mother reacts by saying *'Oh look! I didn't know our cat could fly.'* *Own answer*
5) The author turns into an ant and Dad turns into a mouse.
6) Tibby the cat lives in the house. *Own answer*

Objective focus
1)

Part of story	What happens
Beginning	Mum spills magic on the cat
Middle	The cat grows wings, flies and turns Mum into a snail.
End	The author turns into an ant, Dad turns into a mouse and the cat lives in the house.

2), 3) *Own answer*

Links to writing
1), 2) *Own answers*

17 Planning your story
Comprehension
1) A soup factory. He was called Ashley.
2) He fell into a vat of tomato soup.
3) A daring diver.
4) It was infected by radioactive cosmic dust.
5) To draw the reader's attention and make the story more interesting.
6) It tells you the story continues.

Objective focus
1) *Own answer*
2)

Beginning	Introduces the main character.
Middle	Tells us how he became soup boy.
End	We don't know.

3), 4) *Own answers*

Links to writing
1), 2) *Own answers*

18 Endings
Comprehension
1) Little Red Riding Hood
2) Little Red Riding Hood, the Big Bad Wolf and Grandmother. Yes, because they act the same as in the fairy tale.
3) *Own answer*
4) Singing or talking rhythmically with rhyming words.
5) Yes, some of the words rhyme: 'wood' and 'hood', 'away' and 'day', 'bed' and 'red'.
6) The events happen much more quickly and there is not much description.

Objective focus
2) *Own answer*
1)

	What happens
Beginning	Introduced to Red Riding Hood and how she plans to visit grandmother.
Middle	Introduced the Big Bad Wolf and how he plans to eat her.

3) just, so, till, and, then

Links to writing
1), 2) *Own answers*

19 Time and place
Comprehension
1) Dad says, *'It's your first time out.'*
2) The boy looks lost and the bushes are thicker.
3) summer
4) The amount of light in the sky.
5) The pictures help us.
6) The story shows the progression of one day from morning to evening.

Objective focus
1)

Picture	The place	The time
1	his house – outside	early morning
2	open countryside	late morning
3	edge of wood	midday
4	in the woods	twilight
5	in a puddle, field	early evening
6	home	late evening

2), 3) *Own answers*

Links to writing
1), 2) *Own answers*

20 Paragraphs
Comprehension
1) A short tale to teach a moral lesson, often using personified animals or inanimate objects as the main characters.
2) Yes, this fable uses the Sun and Wind as the main characters. The Sun *'smiled'*. *'The Wind thought he was more powerful.'*
3) They were deciding who was stronger.
4) The Sun is *'all fire'* and *'can destroy anything'* it wants. The Wind is *'all strength and force'*.
5) Whoever can make a man take his coat off fastest.
6) The Wind *'blew and blew'* trying *'to tear the coat from the man's back'*. The Sun *'shone down on the man'* and won the challenge.

Objective focus
1)

Paragraph	Detail in it
1	The main characters. They have an argument.
2	The Sun demonstrates his power.
3	The Wind demonstrates his power.
4	A farmer suggests a final challenge.
5	They agree to the challenge.
6	The Wind fails.
7	The Sun is victorious.
8	The moral of the story.

2) Yes, a new paragraph should begin when the time, setting, or scene changes or when a new character starts speaking.
3) A crow was dying of thirst. He saw a big jug of water on the ground. When he came up to it, there was only a little water in the bottom. He tried to overturn the jug, but it was too heavy.
At last he saw some small stones. He threw them into the jug until the water level rose. He then drank to his heart's content.
This proves that if you are clever you will be successful in the end.

Links to writing
1) *Own answer*

21 Beginning new paragraphs
Comprehension
1) He visited because he is studying Invaders and Settlers in history.
2) Romans, Anglo-Saxons and Vikings.
3) They came in the 8th century to the 12th century AD.
4) Boudicca fought the Romans and was killed.
5) Vikings didn't wear helmets with horns and Roman soldiers didn't like Britain because it was too cold.
6) Yes, each paragraph is about a single topic with a topic sentence telling us what the paragraph will be about, followed by sentences telling us more about the topic sentence.

Objective focus
1) The topic sentence introduces the paragraph and tells the reader what the paragraph will be about.
2) 'To make toast with a toaster is very easy' is the topic sentence because it introduces the paragraph and lets you know what the paragraph will be about.
To make toast with a toaster is very easy.
Before you can switch it on, you need to push down the handle so the bread goes into the toaster.
Switch it on.
You'll need to turn the dial on the toaster to the right time.
Place some bread in the slots in the toaster.
When the toast is ready, it will pop up.

Links to writing
1), 2) *Own answers*

23 Full stops or commas?
Comprehension
1) Grey Rabbit says, '*What a lovely birthday it has been*'.
2) '*They all laughed and sang and danced till night came*'
3) Grey Rabbit says, '*How kind everybody is to me*'.
4) Wise Owl, Mrs Hedgehog, Fuzzypeg and Water Rat
5) It plays the song of the nightingale.
6) A real nightingale answered.

Objective focus
1) *Own answer*. It makes less sense because there are no separations.
2) Fred looked around. He did not know what to do. He felt very miserable and alone. Fred decided to walk towards the sea. He sat down in the sand under a palm tree. Our hero was so tired he fell asleep.
3) **a.** I collect stamps, coins, trains and stickers.
   b. His favourite colours were red, green, blue and orange.
   c. The four seasons are autumn, winter, spring and summer.

Links to writing
1), 2) *Own answers*

24 Punctuation of speech
Comprehension
1) She had a very loud voice.
2) She '*startled the midwife*', '*astonished the neighbours*' and '*frightened the birds*'.
3) It got louder.
4) So that her voice would be quieter outside the house.
5) To emphasise them being loud.
6) Sending her to boarding school.

Objective focus
1) Three from:
   "We can only hope," said her mother as she covered her ears with embroidered pillows.
   "GOOD MORNING!" Emily said in her Emily voice.
   "Please be soft," said her father.
   "GOOD AFTERNOON!" Emily said in her Emily voice.
2) **a.** Fred said, "I feel happy today."
   b. "My team didn't win again," sighed Ranjit.
   c. "Have you ever been to Australia?" asked Tracy.
3) **a.** "I want a drink," said Tracy.
   b. "How many sweets have you taken?" asked Fred.
   c. "That's not fair if you've got more money!" said Harry.

Links to writing
1), 2) *Own answer*

25 Using connectives
Comprehension
1) *Own answer*
2) Cycling makes you healthier.
3) More time using a bicycle.
4) Sitting in front of computers.
5) Useful bike information.
6) '*It's often hard to find what you want*' about biking.

Objective focus
1) Without connectives, the passage would be very jerky and difficult to read. Connectives help the writing flow.
2) **a.** She put up her umbrella because it was raining.
   b. I tried hard, but I could not do it.
   c. I hurt my arm when I was playing rugby.

Links to writing
1) *Own answer*

26 Writing sentences using adjectives
Comprehension
1) So she could get outside quickly to play in the snow.
2) Because the scarf was itchy.
3) '**thick**' and '**soft**'
4) She '*poked her finger into the clean snow*'.
5) *Own answer*
6) dizzy

Objective focus
1), 2), 3) *Own answers*

Links to writing
1), 2) *Own answers*

27 Writing sentences using verbs
Comprehension
1) '*He lived over the hill behind the town*'.
2) He blew the smoke down into the mill and it was unpopular because the men '*coughed*' and '*spluttered*'.
3) He rang the schoolhouse bell half an hour early. The children would not have liked this because they would have had to rush their breakfast and arrive early for school.
4) The waves the Giant caused swamped his boats or smashed them on the bank.
5) The giant could lean over into a chimney, he could reach the schoolhouse bell and he made great waves in the river. *Own answer*

Objective focus
1), 2), 3) *Own answers*

Links to writing
1), 2) *Own answers*

Author: Andrew Plaistowe

Comprehension

1) From where does Mr Croc get the idea to do some exercise?

2) What three kinds of exercises does he do?

3) How does he realise that he should not eat before exercising?

4) How does the reader know that time has passed?

5) Why are people looking strangely at him at the end of the story?

6) What do you think the joke is behind the cartoon story?

Objective focus

1) Make a chart of the order of events in the story.

Event	Time in story	What happens
1		
2		

2) Tell the story with the events in a different order. What happens? Decide if there is a correct order to the events in this story. Explain why.

3) Make three boxes with these headings. Sort the events of this story into the correct box.

Beginning of story	Middle of story	End of story

Links to writing

1) Draw another cartoon story about Mr Croc and what he gets up to. Use speech bubbles. Fit the whole story on to one page. Decide upon the correct order for your story. What comes first? What comes next? How does the story end?

2) Imagine you are making a film of your cartoon. You could write a script and draw pictures. You need to be more detailed. Think about the middle of your story.

How do you build up the story? What is the problem?

Show how you solved the problem.

Carry on to the end of your story.

16 Beginnings

Let's look at how stories begin.

Magic Cat

My mum whilst walking through the door
Spilt some magic on the floor.
Blobs of this
And splots of that
But most of it upon the cat.

Our cat turned magic, straight away
And in the garden went to play
Where it grew two massive wings
And flew around in fancy rings.
'Oh look!' cried Mother, pointing high,
'I didn't know our cat could fly.'
Then with a dash of Tibby's tail
She turned my mum into a snail!

She now lives beneath a stone
And dusts around a different home.
And I'm an ant
And Dad's a mouse
And Tibby's living in our house.

Peter Dixon

Chat challenge

Does every story have a beginning? If so, why?

What would stories be like if they did not have a beginning?

Does the beginning of your story always have to start with the first thing that happened?

Where else can you start a story?

Does a beginning always have to be exciting?

Comprehension

1) Name the four characters in this story.

2) Who causes the problem in the first place?

3) What happens to the cat? Which words tell you how fast it happened?

4) What is the mother's reaction? Do you find this surprising? Explain why.

5) What becomes of the author and Dad?

6) What's the final joke about the cat? Do you think it's funny? Give your reasons.

Objective focus

1) Copy and complete the chart. Show what happens in the story.

Part of story	What happens?
Beginning	
Middle	
End	

2) Write two other beginnings which might have caused this problem. You do not have to write in poetry. Compare these with others in the class. How are they different? Did they start with action or description?

3) Look at reading books in the class. How do they begin? Carry out a survey about story beginnings. Which is the most popular? Do certain kinds of stories have the same beginnings?

Links to writing

1) Tell the beginning of 'Magic Cat', but not as a poem. Use description and speech.

   How will you open the story? Action? Speech? Description?

   What will the setting be?

   What does the character do? How does Mum react? How does the cat react?

   Which other characters are present? How do they react?

2) Imagine you are making a film of the poem. You could write a script and draw pictures.

   How do you build up the story? What is the problem?

   Show how you solved the problem. Carry on to the end of your story.

17 Planning your story

Let's look at a very strange story to see how it is planned.

From *Soupy Boy*

On a visit to a soup factory with his parents, he fell into a vat of tomato soup!

Into the soup the daring diver dove. HOWEVER, this wasn't just any old soup, oh no! Unknown to all, this soup was infected by RADIOACTIVE COSMIC DUST! And so, by the time Ashley was fished out, he'd mutated into...

Damon Burnard

Chat challenge

Why is it important to plan your stories before you write them?

What would happen when you had written about your first few good ideas?

What might a plan for your story look like?

Is it important to have a beginning? A middle? An end? Why?

Comprehension

1) Where was the hero of our story visiting when the accident happened? What was he called?

2) What happened to him there?

3) Who volunteers to rescue the boy?

4) Why was the soup dangerous?

5) Why do you think some words are written in capital letters in a different typeface?

6) What do the last three dots on the page tell you about the story?

Objective focus

1) Look at the title of the story. Write about what you think will be in this story, e.g. *superhero*, *fighting villain*, *disguise*, etc.

2) How is this story planned? Copy and complete the chart to help.

Beginning	
Middle	
End	We don't know!

3) Look at what you are told in this unit about the story. Make notes on:

   a. opening   **b.** characters   **c.** problem

4) Now make notes about what you think will happen in the rest of the story:

   a. dealing with problem   **b.** solving the problem   **c.** the end

Links to writing

1) Write the story after the passage ends.

   Use drawings and speech bubbles.

   Use a computer to change important words into different typefaces.

2) Write a story of your own child superhero.

   What will he or she be called?

   What will the plan of your story be like?

18 Endings

Let's investigate how and why stories end.

Big Bad Raps

Just on the edge
of a deep, dark wood
lived a girl called
Little Red Riding Hood.
Her grandmother lived
not far away,
so Red went to pay her a
visit one day …

And the Big Bad Wolf,
who knew her plan
he turned his nose
and ran and ran.
He ran till he came
to her grandmother's door.

Then he locked her up
with a great big roar.
He took her place
in her nice warm bed,
and he waited there
for Little Miss Red.

Tony Mitton

Chat challenge

Does every story have an ending?
What would your audience think if there wasn't one?
Does a story always have to end 'happily ever after'?
How else can stories end?

Comprehension

1) What traditional story does this poem use?

2) Which characters are in it? Are they behaving in the way you would expect? Explain why.

3) Explain what happens in the traditional story as you know it.

4) What is a **rap**? What features do you expect a rap to have?

5) Does this poem contain these features? Explain how.

6) How is this version of the traditional story different?

Objective focus

1) Copy and complete the chart to say what happens in each part of the story.

What happens?	
Beginning	
Middle	
End	We don't know

2) Do you know the ending to this story? Make a list of what has to happen in the story to get to the right ending.
   What happens if you miss anything out? Do the facts have to be in a certain order?

3) Identify some of the connectives in the poem that let the story follow a particular order, e.g. *Just … so …*

Links to writing

1) Continue this story, but not in poetry. Give it a 'happily ever after' ending for young children. Then write another ending, but more bloodthirsty, for children of your age. Would this still be 'happily ever after'?
   How will you make sure your story follows steps, so your reader can understand the end?
   How will you make time pass?
   How will you make the story exciting, but not give too much away?

2) Choose another fairy story or traditional tale. Write the story, but give it a very different ending.

19 Time and place

What do you understand by **place** in a story?

Are all stories set in a place? Say why.

Do all stories give you a sense of the time of day or time of year?

How do they do this?

Comprehension

1) How do you know the boy has not been out on his bike before?

2) When he gets to the countryside, how do you guess that he is lost?

3) In what time of the year is this story set?

4) How do we know what time of day it is in each picture?

5) There are few words in this story. How do we know what happens to the boy?

6) How do you know that time has passed in this story?

Objective focus

1) Look at each picture. Using a chart like this one, explain what each tells us about the place and the time.

Picture	The place	The time
1	his house – outside	early morning

2) The story is set in the countryside. Write a list of words to describe it. Use a chart about your senses to help.

Seeing	Hearing	Touching	Smelling	Tasting
	birds singing		flowers	

3) List the detail in the passage about the place.

Picture	What it tells me	Which senses does it appeal to? Why?	How does it make me feel?
dark clouds – thunder and lightning	storm	hearing, seeing, can feel the rain	scared, frightened

Links to writing

1) Now turn the cartoon into a story in paragraphs. You could write one paragraph for each picture.

2) Write a description of your school and its playground at lunchtime. Start with quiet. Then make it noisy and busy. Go back to silent again.
   Make notes about what you can see, feel, hear, taste and touch.
   Describe the details of what the place looks like.
   What will the weather be like? This will make a difference to your senses.
   How will you show time passing?

20 Paragraphs

The Sun and the Wind

It was not a happy day in Ancient Greece. The Sun and the Wind were having an argument. People on the ground were scared. They could not get on with their farming. The Sun and the Wind were deciding who was the strongest.

"I am the most powerful," said the Sun. "I am all fire. I can destroy anything I want". He pointed a few rays at a tree. It burst into flames. He smiled. The people hid.

The Wind thought he was more powerful. "I am all strength and force," he said. He blew gently. The people smiled as the leaves rustled. He blew strongly and a tree fell to the ground. People ran and hid. The wind smiled.

A farmer on the ground was tired of this. He shouted up, "Why don't you have one last challenge to prove who is the strongest? At least the people of the Earth would then be safe."

The Sun and the Wind stared each other out. After a time, they knew they must agree. A small, dark man walked by. They decided to use him as a test. "Whoever can make him take off his coat the fastest will win," said the Sun.

So, the Wind blew and blew. He tried to tear the coat from the man's back. But the man just hugged the coat to himself even more and struggled on.

The Sun decided to be gentle in his approach. He shone down on the man. Suddenly the man started to become very hot. He puffed and panted. He sweated. So what did he do? He took off his coat.

The Sun had won the battle. But what is the moral of this story? The Sun won the challenge not by being fierce and violent, but by being gentle and persistent. You could try that as well.

Aesop

Chat challenge

What is a **paragraph**?
Why is it important to write in paragraphs?
What would happen if you didn't?
How do you know when to start a new paragraph?

Comprehension

1) What is a **fable**? What feature should a fable always have?

2) Does this fable have this? Find the evidence.

3) What was the argument between the Sun and the Wind about?

4) Explain why each of them thought they were the most powerful.

5) What test were they set?

6) How did each of them do to try to win? Who won in the end?

Objective focus

1) Make notes about what detail is in each paragraph. A chart might help.

Paragraph	Detail in it
1	The main characters. They have an argument.

2) Is every paragraph about something different? Write a rule about when you should use a new paragraph.

3) Here is another one of Aesop's fables. Write it out correctly in paragraphs, following your rule. Talk with others about whether they have something different and why.

A crow was dying of thirst. He saw a big jug of water on the ground. When he came up to it, there was only a little water in the bottom. He tried to overturn the jug, but it was too heavy. At last he saw some small stones. He threw them into the jug until the water level rose. He then drank to his heart's content. This proves that if you are clever you will be successful in the end.

Links to writing

1) Here are some notes about another fable called *The Fox and the Crow*. Use these notes. Follow the events in order to write clear paragraphs. Add details to make an atmosphere. Don't forget the setting! What's the moral of the story?

crow → stole piece of cheese → flew into tree → cheese in beak → fox came by → hungry → spoke to crow → no cheese → flattered crow → said had nice voice → said was beautiful → crow sang → cheese fell out of beak to ground → fox ran away with it → may have been beautiful → no brains!

21 Beginning new paragraphs

Jamie has written all about his visit to the British Museum. Has he used paragraphs correctly?

We went on a school visit to the British Museum. The reason is because we are doing Invaders and Settlers in history. People who invaded Britain and then lived here were the Romans, the Anglo-Saxons and the Vikings.

First we went to see the rooms about Vikings. They came in the 8th century AD until around 1100. Vikings were warriors. People were scared of them.

> This is the topic sentence. It tells us what the paragraph will be about.

Then we went to see the Romans. They came to Britain in AD 43. Boudicca fought the Romans but lost. She was killed.

> Connectives (in red) tell us about how to order paragraphs.

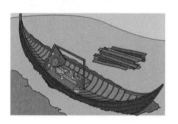

After that we went to see the Anglo-Saxon Sutton Hoo ship burial. They found lots of treasure from the 7th century AD there.

> The sentences tell us more about the topic sentence.

I learned a lot from my visit to the British Museum. The best thing I learned was that Vikings didn't really wear helmets with horns like they do in the films. I also learned that the Roman soldiers didn't like it here. It was too cold for them. Finally, I found out that Anglo-Saxon words are still here in place names.

Chat challenge

What is a **paragraph**?
What is a **topic sentence**?
Why are they important to your reader?
How do you know when to start a new paragraph?
What other words show you the correct order of the paragraphs?

Comprehension

1) Why did Jamie visit the British Museum?

2) Which people invaded Britain and lived here?

3) When did the Vikings come to Britain?

4) Who fought the Romans? What happened to her?

5) List two things that Jamie learned from his visit.

6) Do you think Jamie has used paragraphs correctly? Say why.

Objective focus

1) Explain how the topic sentences, in bold, tell you what else is going to be in the paragraph.

2) These sentences are about making toast. They are not in the right order. Put them in the right order. Write the paragraph. Which is your topic sentence? How do you know?

Before you can switch it on, you need to push down the handle so the bread goes into the toaster.
Place some bread in the slots in the toaster.
You'll need to turn the dial on the toaster to the right time.
When the toast is ready, it will pop up.
Switch it on.
To make toast with a toaster is very easy.

Links to writing

1) Here is a plan for a piece of writing: 'My favourite TV programme'.

Paragraph 1	The sorts of programmes I like and why
Paragraph 2	My favourite programme and what it's about
Paragraph 3	Characters – who I like and don't like – and why
Paragraph 4	My favourite episode
Paragraph 5	Why it's better than others – why it's different

Write the first sentence for each paragraph.

2) Choose one paragraph. Write the paragraph under your topic sentence.

**Assess your
understanding** OK   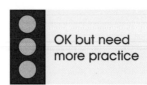 OK but need
more practice    not at all clear
and need to
revisit

22 What have we learned?

We've learned how to **create and shape texts** and about **text structure and
organisation**.

1 How to explore story order

● There is always a beginning, a middle and an end.

   – In a better story there is a beginning, a buildup, a problem, a resolution and an ending.

● A story always has a setting, characters and a theme.

Check understanding!

 Check one of your own stories. Is there a clear order? How could you improve it?

2 How to write a good beginning

● All stories/poems have a beginning so make it a good one!

● Include characters, the setting and a problem.

● Start with different ideas: use speech, description, action.

Check understanding!

 Choose one of your own stories. Rewrite the beginning at least three times.

3 How to plan a story

Stories don't just happen so you need to plan:

● Beginning: characters, setting, problem/theme

● Middle: buildup, problem, resolution

● End: finish off ideas and round it off.

Check understanding!

 Find three short story books. In the first find the main characters, the setting and the
theme. In the second find the buildup, problem and the resolution. In the third find
the end.

Assess your understanding OK 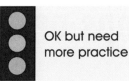 OK but need more practice not at all clear and need to revisit

4 How to write a good ending

- All stories/poems have an end so make it a good one!
- Finish off ideas unless you are deliberately finishing with a **?**
- Finish with different ideas:

  – a character reflecting on the events – speech   – with an answer

  – with action   – happily

  – with a mystery   – sadly.

Check understanding!

 Choose one of your own stories. Rewrite the ending at least three times.

5 How to use language for signalling time and place

- Be clear about when and where the story takes place. Introduce the setting.
- Use objects, the seasons or time to tell the reader when the story is set.
- Use the five senses to tell the reader where it is set.

Check understanding!

 Describe a setting: one using an object, one using a season and one using time to describe where a story is set.

6 How to use paragraphs well

- Paragraphs help readers to follow the story.
- In stories begin a new paragraph when:

  – the time changes   – the scene changes

  – the setting changes   – there is a new event

  – the speaker changes in a section of speech   – a new character appears.

Check understanding!

 Read two paragraphs of your reading book. At the end of each paragraph, make a note of the main focus.

23 Full stops or commas?

Can you decide when to use full stops or commas? Here is a passage from a book for very young children.

From *Little Grey Rabbit's Birthday*

They all laughed and sang and danced till night came, and then they went home by the light of the moon.

"What a lovely birthday it has been," said Grey Rabbit. "How kind everybody is to me."

She looked at her presents on the table: the musical box with the song of the nightingale, Wise Owl's 'Guide to Knowledge', a handkerchief from Mrs Hedgehog, a tiny chestnut basket of flowers from Fuzzypeg, a little canoe from Water Rat, the feather fan, the puff-ball purse, the honey pots, and all the other little treasures.

She went upstairs to bed, with the musical box under her arm. She turned the handle and the voice of the nightingale came trilling forth. From the woods another nightingale answered.

Alison Uttley

Chat challenge

What is a **full stop**?
What is a **comma**?
How are they different?
Why is it important to use them both correctly in your writing?

Comprehension

1) How do you know what Grey Rabbit was celebrating?

2) How do you know that she was having a party?

3) How did Grey Rabbit feel about her friends once they had gone home?

4) List the characters in the story who had given Grey Rabbit presents.

5) What was special about her music box?

6) What happened when it played?

Objective focus

1) Write out the paragraph where Grey Rabbit describes what she got for her birthday but do not include any commas. Read it. Does it make sense? Why not?

2) Put the full stops in this passage.

   Fred looked around he did not know what to do he felt very miserable and alone Fred decided to walk towards the sea he sat down in the sand under a palm tree our hero was so tired he fell asleep

   Remember: when do you need capital letters?

3) Put the commas in these sentences:

   a. I collect stamps coins trains and stickers.

   b. His favourite colours were red green blue and orange.

   c. The four seasons are autumn winter spring and summer.

Links to writing

1) Imagine you won the lottery. What would you buy for yourself? Write a list starting 'I would buy: …'.

   Use commas correctly in the list.

   Use an adjective to describe each noun in your list.

2) Write about yourself for the school website. Punctuate your sentences correctly.

   a. My name is … Five things I'm good at are …

   b. The foods I like most are …

   c. The three things I hate most are …

   etc.

24 Punctuation of speech

Can you decide how and when to punctuate speech?

From *Loud Emily*

From the moment of birth Emily's voice boomed.

"GOO GOO BA BA!" Emily sang in her Emily voice.

It startled the midwife. It astonished the neighbours. It frightened the birds that were nesting in trees.

Emily's parents loved her truly, but oh, dear! Her voice could be heard 'round that seaside town!

"Perhaps she'll grow out of it," said her father as he closed all the windows and fastened all the doors.

"We can only hope," said her mother as she covered her ears with embroidered pillows.

But as Emily grew, so did her voice. It rattled the brasses. It shimmied the crystals. It shattered the plates as they crashed to the floor.

"**GOOD MORNING!**" Emily said in her Emily voice.

"Please be soft," said Father.

"**GOOD AFTERNOON!**" Emily said in her Emily voice.

"What about a boarding school?" her father wondered.

Alexis O'Neill

Chat challenge

Why is it important to use the correct punctuation when you write someone's words?

How is it different from other punctuation?

Which words do you put inside these punctuation marks?

What rules do you know about punctuating speech?

Comprehension

1) What was special about Emily?

2) When she was born, what three different reactions does the author give?

3) What happened to her voice as she got older?

4) Why did her father close all the doors and windows?

5) Why do you think the author has written certain words in capital letters?

6) What was her parents' solution to Emily's loud voice?

Objective focus

1) Write three examples of speech in the passage. Underline the words inside speech marks.

2) Write these correctly. Put the correct words in speech marks.

   a. Fred said, I feel happy today.

   b. My team didn't win again, sighed Ranjit.

   c. Have you ever been to Australia, asked Tracy.

3) Look at these examples. Find the ones where the punctuation is wrong and correct them.

   a. "I want a drink" said Tracy

   b. "How many sweets have you taken" asked Fred

   c. "That's not fair if you've got more money" said Harry

Links to writing

1) Draw a cartoon story about Emily at boarding school. Use speech bubbles.

   What happens when she arrives? How do people react?
   What happens because of her loud voice?

2) Write this passage correctly punctuated. Underline the words the characters say before you start. Remember to put each new speaker on a new line.

   two men had just won the lottery I feel a bit hungry I'll buy some pies said one that's great said the other as they were eating their pies they passed a motor showroom I've always wanted a Rolls Royce said one I'll buy a couple said his friend no said the first man these are on me you bought the pies

25 Using connectives

Can you decide *how* and *when* to use connectives?

| One piece of information | *This connective just joins one piece of information to another.* | Another piece of information |

The car was going very fast AND I didn't see it.

| One piece of information | *This connective says that something else was possible. It **adds** information.* | Extra information |

It was heading straight for me BUT he didn't realise I was fast on my bike.

| One piece of information | *This connective gives us **a reason** for something.* | This is the reason for or the result of the first piece of information. |

I think I am alive today BECAUSE I went to road safety lessons.

Cycling is fun **and** it is healthy. School work can keep you busy **but** we want you to spend more time pedalling, **and** less time sitting in front of the computer. Our site lists useful bike stuff on the Internet **because** it's often hard to find what you want. It's easy to find the information out there **when** someone helps you. It's free and it's interesting **so** why aren't you finding out more?

www.bikeforall.net

Chat challenge

What is a **connective**?
What do connectives connect?
What kind of words are connectives?
What would happen in sentences if you did not use them?

Comprehension

1) Which words do you not understand? Look them up in a dictionary.

2) Give one reason why cycling is good for you.

3) What does the writer really mean when she says 'more time pedalling'?

4) What does she think young people spend most of their time doing?

5) What is on their Internet site?

6) Why might it be useful?

Objective focus

1) Read the passage without the connectives. What difference does it make? What do connectives do in sentences?

2) Make these pairs of sentences into one sentence. Choose the best connective.

   a. She put up her umbrella. It was raining. **and but because**

   b. I tried hard. I could not do it. **and so but**

   c. I hurt my arm. I was playing rugby. **after when and**

Links to writing

1) Choose connectives from the box to go in these gaps. Compare your answers with a friend. Do different connectives make the sentences mean something different?

   a. He slept through the show … he missed the end.

   b. You will get no pocket money … you begin to tidy your bedroom.

   c. I liked the story of the film … the acting was dreadful.

   d. She worked hard for a term … she came top in the exams.

   e. You only stand a chance to win … you buy a lottery ticket.

and	but
so	because
when	after
while	since
until	unless
although	

26 Writing sentences using adjectives

Let's investigate *how* and *when* to use adjectives when writing sentences.

From *Josie Smith at Christmas*

Josie Smith ate her breakfast as fast as she could and then she put her coat and wellingtons on and her **itchy** scarf and went out in the yard.

The snow in the yard was **thick** and **soft** and the **knobbly black** stones of the walls had **little** slices of snow in all their cracks. Josie Smith poked her finger into the **clean** snow and tasted some. Then she made some footprints right across the middle and walked back in them and made them go back to front. Then she stood still with her face to the sky. The snowflakes were twirling round and round and round and round right up as far as the top of the sky and they made Josie Smith feel dizzy. She shut her eyes and let the **big** snowflakes land on her face and tickle and burn and melt. It was very quiet. She pulled her tongue out and a snowflake melted there.

Magdalen Nabb

Chat challenge

What is an **adjective**?
What kind of word do they describe?
Why is it important to use them in your writing?
What would happen to your reader's interest if you did not use them?

Comprehension

1) Why do you think Josie ate her breakfast so fast?

2) Why might she not have liked wearing her scarf?

3) Write down two adjectives that the author uses to describe the snow.

4) What did Josie do to taste the snow?

5) Explain what she did with her footprints. Why do you think she did this?

6) When she looked at the snow falling, how did this make her feel?

Objective focus

1) Write out some sentences without the adjectives, e.g. 'Josie *put on her scarf*'. What difference does it make? What information is left out?

2) Add two or three adjectives to the nouns in these boring sentences, e.g. '*The man walked down the road.*' → '*The tall, thin man walked down the long, dark road.*'

   a. The man walked down the road. The girls pushed the car.

   b. The boy cleaned his shoes. The elephant ran through the jungle.

   c. He put on a clean shirt.

3) **Nice** is an overused adjective. Think of adjectives that you could use instead of **nice** that would have the same meaning. Write the sentences.

   a. a nice jacket   b. a nice cottage   c. a nice meal

   d. a nice film   e. a nice holiday   f. a nice dog

Links to writing

1) Continue Josie's description of being in the snow. What did she do next? What was it like? Use adjectives to describe what she feels, sees, touches, tastes and hears.

2) Collect adjectives under these headings to describe: a fox, a tortoise, a lion, a snake, an owl.

Shape	Size	Colour	Texture

Write sentences containing some of these adjectives.

27 Writing sentences using verbs

Let's investigate how and when to use verbs in your writing.

In this story, the Giant is acting very badly …

From *The Gigantic Badness*

He **lived** over the hill behind the town, but sometimes he **crossed** the field where the saw-mill was and if the smoke **was** coming out of the tall chimney he **leaned** over and **blew** down it so that the men who **were working** in the mill **coughed** and **spluttered**.

Sometimes in the early morning he reached a finger to the schoolhouse bell hanging high against the roof, and all the children, halfway through their breakfasts, gulped and gobbled and raced into school half an hour early. Once when Tom was sailing his boats in the river the Giant decided it was a good day to take a swim farther upstream, and he enjoyed it so much that he lay on his back, kicking and splashing. Water rose up round him in fountains, and then poured downstream in great waves, so that Tom's boats were swamped, and those that didn't sink were tossed against the bank with their rigging tangled and the thin stick masts smashed into pieces. That was bad enough, but a week later while Tom was out on the hill flying his new kite the Giant walked by, tangling the string of the kite in his bootlaces so that the kite came down in the middle of a gorse bush, all torn and broken.

Janet McNeill

Chat challenge

What is a **verb**?
Why is it important to use them in your writing?
Can you write sentences without them? Give examples.
Why is it important not to use the same verbs time and time again?

Comprehension

1) Where did the Giant live?

2) What did he do at the mill? Why would this have been unpopular?

3) What did he do at the school? Do you think the children would have liked this? Explain why.

4) Why was Tom so annoyed with the Giant when he played with his boats?

5) How does the author give you a sense of how big the Giant is compared to Tom? Where does it tell you this?

Objective focus

1) Look at what the verbs in this passage tell us.

> Sometimes in the early morning he reached a finger to the schoolhouse bell *hanging* high against the roof, and all the children, halfway through their breakfasts, *gulped* and *gobbled* and *raced* into school half an hour early.

Use different verbs from the ones above. How does it change what we understand, e.g. do **gulped** and **gobbled** tell us how quickly they ate?

2) Use a thesaurus. Collect ten verbs which you could use instead of each of these weaker verbs. Use them in sentences.

   a. to walk   **b.** he ate   **c.** we went

3) Make the verbs in these phrases more exciting, e.g. **coming** *could be* **puffing, pouring, gushing**.

   a. the smoke was **coming** out of the tall chimney   **b.** **blew** down it

   c. the Giant **decided** it was a good day

Links to writing

1) Write about how Tom got his revenge against the Giant. Make the story more exciting by using vivid verbs to describe actions.

   What happened to make Tom really mad? Describe this.

   What did he decide to do? How did he do it?

   How did the Giant react? What happens in the end?

2) Use these verbs instead of **said**. Explain how they all mean different things. Write some speech using them.

   shouted   whispered   questioned   argued   wondered

Assess your understanding

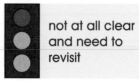

OK

OK but need more practice

not at all clear and need to revisit

28 What have we learned?

We've learned about **sentence structure and punctuation**.

1 How to use full stops and commas

- Sentences begin with a capital letter and end with a full stop (**.**), question mark (**?**) or exclamation mark (**!**).

- A comma (**,**) splits parts of a sentence and it is used:

  – in a list to separate names or items

  – to add a bit of information into a sentence, e.g. *My sister, Ellen Rose, loves chocolate spread.*

  – to add a bit of information after a subordinate clause, e.g. *Even though Evie was tired, she still finished her homework.*

Check understanding!

 Write out a shopping list for a party.

Include a **!** and a **?** somewhere in your plan.

2 How to punctuate speech

- Speech marks can look like this: '...', or like this: "...".

- Use a capital letter inside the speech mark, e.g. 'Cool,' said Tim.

- When a new character speaks begin on a new line.

Check understanding!

 Write out a conversation you have had today (or make one up).

Include no more than three characters. Show the speech marks clearly.

Assess your understanding

 OK

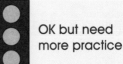 OK but need more practice

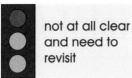 not at all clear and need to revisit

3 How to use connectives

- Use connectives in fiction and non-fiction writing.

- Connectives to join sentences together: **and, but, although**.

- Causal connectives: **because, so, since, unless**.

- Time connectives: **when, while, until, first, next, finally**.

Check understanding!

 Look through some books. How many connectives can you find in three minutes? Test some friends to see if they can find more in the time.

4 How to write sentences using adjectives

- An adjective is a word that describes somebody or something.

- Adjectives come before a noun, e.g. **the pretty dog**, *or after some verbs like* **be, get, seem, feel, look**, e.g. *The cat looks scary.*

- Try not to repeat the same adjective, e.g. *It was a nice place in a nice part of town on a nice day.*

Check understanding!

 Look through some books. Find as many adjectives as you can in three minutes. Test some friends to see if they can find more in the time.

5 How to write sentences using verbs

- A verb is a word that tells us about an action, about something that has happened or about a process. It can be a **doing** or a **being** word.

- Every sentence needs a verb.

- Verbs can sometimes improve your writing more than by just adding adjectives and adverbs.

Check understanding!

 Find five sentences from your own work or from a book.

Rewrite them using different and better verbs.

Helpful Year 3 words

adjective   a word that usually comes before a noun and gives us more detail about it

adverb   a word that usually comes after a verb and tells us how the action of the verb is being done

apostrophe   a punctuation mark (') used to indicate possession, e.g. *Jo's cat*. It can also be used to indicate the omission of letters or numbers, e.g. *It's time to go.*

calligrams   a word that is written in a way that matches its meaning

characters   people or animals in a story or play

connectives   words that join parts of sentences together

instructions   tell you how to do something in a step-by-step way

narrative   the recounting or telling of past events; account, chronicle, description, list, story, report, statement

paragraph   groups of sentences that are all about the same topic, separated from the rest of the text by a line space above and below, or by indenting the first line (leaving a space between the margin and the first word). A paragraph usually contains sentences that deal with one topic, and a new paragraph signals a change of topic

plural   means more than one of something

prefix   a letter pattern fixed to the beginning of a word which affects its meaning

punctuation   the symbols used in written language to indicate the end of a sentence or a clause, or to indicate that it is a question, etc. **. , ; : ? ! ' - " " ( )** are the punctuation symbols most commonly used in English

reports   non-chronological reports give facts about a subject

shape poetry   poems whose words are written out in the shape of
the subject

singular   means one of something

speech marks   punctuation marks that show us when a character
is speaking

suffix   a letter pattern fixed to the end of a word which affects
its meaning

verb   a word which shows what someone or something is doing

vocabulary   the words we use

Y3 literacy topics

Narrative plays and scripts	stories with familiar settings	myths, legends, fables, traditional tales	adventure and mystery	authors and letters	dialogue and plays
Non-fiction	reports		instructions		information texts
Poetry	poems to perform		shape poetry and calligrams		language play

Handy hints

Top tips on spelling
Look, Say, Cover, Write, Check

Look

- Look at the shape of the word.
- Make a picture of the word in your mind.
- Look for tricky bits within the word.

Say

- Say the whole word.
- Say each sound in the word – right through the word.
- Are there are tricky sounds that you need remember?

Cover

- Cover the word.
- Picture the word in your mind.
- Hear the sounds of the word – what were the tricky sounds?

Write

- Write the word.
- Think about the picture in your mind as you write it.
- Say the sounds of the word as you write them.

Check

- Check it.
- If it isn't right then underline the bit you got wrong and try it again!

What helps you most – the look, the sounds or the writing out of the word?

Try to learn these tricky words using the steps above.

after	could	many	said	two
again	eight	once	some	where
because	laugh	people	their	were

Vocabulary

Top tips on vocabulary

1) Don't keep using the same words over and over again because it makes your writing very dull.

2) Every time you want to use **said**, try to think of a different verb to make it more interesting for your reader.

3) Don't use **okay**, **great**, **nice**, **really** and **boring** in your writing.

4) Don't avoid using interesting words just because you aren't sure of the spelling – just have a try!

Presentation

Top tips on handwriting

1) Make sure that your pen or pencil is comfortable (and that the pencil is sharp).

2) Use an eraser (rubber) if you make a mistake.

3) If **you** can't read it then others won't be able to!

4) Try to keep it neat all the time.

And …

Use capital letters for:

- people's names

- people's titles (like Mrs Jones)

- places

- days of the week

- months of the year

And …

Use a full stop at the end of a sentence unless you are using a **?** or a **!**

Rising Stars UK Ltd, 7 Hatchers Mews, Bermondsey Street, London SE1 3GS

www.risingstars-uk.com

Acknowledgements

Page 12 – Photograph by Wig Worland © Wig Worland

Page 14 – From *The Girl Who Stayed for Half a Week* by Gene Kemp, from Roundabout, Faber and Faber 1993

Page 20 – Leaflet: Rutland Water Butterfly Farm

Page 24 – Extract from *Charmed Life* by Diana Wynne Jones, Macmillan and Puffin 1979. © Diana Wynne Jones, 1977. Pemission granted by the author

Page 26 – Extract from 'Secrets' by Anita Desai, published in *Guardian Angels* (ed. Stephanie Nettell), Puffin. Copyright © 1988 Anita Desai. Reproduced by permission of the author c/o Rogers, Coleridge and White Ltd., 20 Powis Mews, London W11 1JN.

Page 28 – 'How Playtime Shapes Up' by Chris Ogden, by permission of author. *What Shape is a Poem?* Chosen by Paul Cookson, Macmillan Children's Books

Page 32 – 'Mr Croc Gets Fit' by Frank Rogers from *Mr Croc,* A&C Black

Page 34 – 'Magic Cat' by Peter Dixon, from Peter Dixon's *Grand Prix of Poetry*, published by Macmillan Children's Books, London, UK

Page 36 – Extract from *Soupy Boy*, by Damon Burnard, Corgi Yearling Books, Transworld

Page 38 – 'Big Bad Raps' by Tony Mitton, Orchard Books

Page 48 – From *Little Grey Rabbit's Birthday* by Alison Uttley, Collins Colour Cubs

Page 50 – 'Loud Emily' by Alexis O'Neill, Simon and Schuster

Page 54 – From *Josie Smith at Christmas* by Magdalen Nabb, Collins Children's Books

Page 56 – 'The Gigantic Badness' by Janet McNeill, from *Bad Boys*, ed Eileen Colwell, Puffin 1972

Every effort has been made to contact copyright holders and obtain their permission for the use of copyright materials. The authors and publisher will gladly receive information enabling them to rectify any error or omission in subsequent editions.

All facts are correct at time of going to press.

Published 2007
Reprinted 2010, 2011 (twice)
Text, design and layout © Rising Stars UK Ltd.

Design: HL Studios and Clive Sutherland
Illustrations: HL Studios
Editorial project management: Dodi Beardshaw
Editorial: Dodi Beardshaw
Cover design: Burville-Riley Partnership

British Library Cataloguing in Publication Data.
A CIP record for this book is available from the British Library.

ISBN: 978-1-84680-092-4

Printed by Craft Print International Ltd, Singapore